We Believe

COMPANION JOURNAL

Copyright © 2026 by Gary Lewis

Published by Arrows & Stones

All rights reserved. No portion of this book may be reproduced, stored in a retrieval system, or transmitted in any form or by any means—electronic, mechanical, photocopy, recording, scanning, or other—except for brief quotations in critical reviews or articles, without prior written permission of the author.

For foreign and subsidiary rights, contact the author.

Cover design by: Sara Young

ISBN: 978-1-969062-11-7   1 2 3 4 5 6 7 8 9 10

Printed in the United States of America

JANUARY

COMPANION JOURNAL

We Believe

A Journey of Faith in Action

GARY LEWIS

CONTENTS

How S.O.A.P Works ix

DAY 1. **January 1** 10

DAY 2. **January 2** 14

DAY 3. **January 3** 17

DAY 4. **January 4** 20

DAY 5. **January 5** 23

DAY 6. **January 6** 26

DAY 7. **January 7** 29

DAY 8. **January 8** 32

DAY 9. **January 9** 35

DAY 10. **January 10** 38

DAY 11. **January 11** 41

DAY 12. **January 12** 44

DAY 13. **January 13** 47

DAY 14. **January 14** 50

DAY 15. **January 15** 53

DAY 16. **January 16** 56

DAY 17. **January 17** 59

DAY 18. **January 18** 62

DAY 19. **January 19** 65

DAY 20. **January 20** 68

DAY 21. **January 21**	71
DAY 22. **January 22**	74
DAY 23. **January 23**	77
DAY 24. **January 24**	80
DAY 25. **January 25**	83
DAY 26. **January 26**	86
DAY 27. **January 27**	89
DAY 28. **January 28**	92
DAY 29. **January 29**	95
DAY 30. **January 30**	98
DAY 31. **January 31**	101

HOW S.O.A.P WORKS

Each day, you will complete a set of prompts using the S.O.A.P. method. S.O.A.P. is a simple way to deepen your time in God's Word.

Start with **Scripture**. Read a passage relevant to the main theme of the day's readings and, if possible, write it down to engage with it more fully.

Next, move to **Observation**: consider what stands out to you in that passage. Is there something in the main message—a word, a phrase, or thought that resonates with you?

Then, shift to **Application**. Ask God how He wants you to apply this truth in your life.

Finally, end with **Prayer**. Lift your needs and pray for others as you invite God to work in your heart through His Word.

JANUARY 1
DAY 1 OF 365

DEVOTIONAL

A new year is a gift, a reminder that God is always in the business of beginnings. When Genesis opens with the words, *"In the beginning God created..."* we are not just reading a historical account—we are being invited to believe in the same God who still speaks light into darkness and breathes life into dust. His first act was creation, and His ongoing desire is re-creation: to restore, renew, and make us whole in His presence.

The story continues in Genesis 2, where God places Adam in the garden and gives him freedom with one command: *"You are free to eat from any tree in the garden; but you must not eat from the tree of the knowledge of good and evil..."* (Genesis 2:16-17). From the very beginning, belief has been tethered to obedience. To believe God is not simply an acknowledgement of His words, but complete trust in those words– enough to shape how we live. Every choice we make this year will reveal whether we believe His voice is life or, instead lean on our own understanding.

The Word even paints a picture of what that life of belief looks like: the righteous are like a tree planted by streams of water, yielding fruit in season, leaves that never wither (Psalm 1:3). Belief roots us. It anchors us in the Word of God and positions us to flourish no matter the storms that may come. This is not mere optimism—it is Spirit-empowered confidence that God's Word produces life wherever it is planted.

Matthew reminds us that God's plan has always been unfolding toward Christ. From the long list of names in Matthew 1:1-17 to the angel's words to Joseph in verse 21—*"You are to give him the name Jesus, because he will save his people from their sins"*—we see the faithfulness of God in every generation. What began in creation finds its fulfillment in Christ. We believe not only in a God who creates, but in a Savior who redeems.

This year, as you walk through the Bible from beginning to end, let every page stir your belief afresh. Don't just read the words—ask the Spirit to ignite them in you. Let them guide your decisions, strengthen your prayers, and renew your worship.

Pray with me:
"Lord, You are the God of beginnings and the God of promises fulfilled. As I step into this year, root me in Your Word like a tree by living water. Fill me with Your Spirit, help me to obey Your voice, and fix my eyes on Jesus, my Savior. I believe, and I give this year into Your hands."

Together, we start the journey declaring: **We Believe.**

TODAY'S READINGS

GENESIS 1   GENESIS 2:1-17   MATTHEW 1:1-25   PSALM 1:1-6

S.O.A.P

SCRIPTURE

OBSERVATION

JANUARY 1 | **13**

APPLICATION

PRAYER

JANUARY 2
DAY 2 OF 365

DEVOTIONAL

God created us for unity and trust (Genesis 2:18-25), yet sin fractured that design when Adam and Eve chose unbelief in the garden (Genesis 3). The same brokenness appears in Cain's jealousy toward Abel, but even in judgment, God marked Cain with mercy (Genesis 4:1-16).

That same choice—to believe or resist—appears in Matthew 2: while the Magi bowed in worship, Herod lashed out in fear. Belief always separates those who receive life from those who reject it.

Psalm 2 reminds us that despite human rage, God's King is already enthroned. Our belief rests in Christ's unshakable reign and His mercy that still reaches into our brokenness.

Today, ask the Spirit to guard your heart from unbelief and to anchor your trust in Jesus, whose redemption is greater than sin.

TODAY'S READINGS

GENESIS 2:18-25   GENESIS 3
GENESIS 4:1-16   MATTHEW 2:1-18   PSALM 2:1-12

S.O.A.P

SCRIPTURE

OBSERVATION

APPLICATION

PRAYER

JANUARY 3

DAY 3 OF 365

DEVOTIONAL

Genesis 4-6 shows both the spread of sin and the thread of faith. While humanity's corruption grieved God, Noah believed and found favor in His eyes. Even in a fallen world, faith set apart those who walked with Him.

In Matthew 2:19-23 and 3, Joseph obeyed God's direction, and John the Baptist prepared the way for Christ, calling people to repentance. True belief always leads to obedience and action, and it declares His protection in the midst of trouble, just as Psalm 3 reminds us: even when surrounded by enemies, God is our shield and the lifter of our heads.

Today, ask the Spirit to strengthen your faith so you can walk in obedience and trust God's covering over your life.

TODAY'S READINGS

GENESIS 4:17-26   GENESIS 5   GENESIS 6
MATTHEW 2:19-23   MATTHEW 3   PSALM 3:1-8

S.O.A.P

SCRIPTURE

OBSERVATION

APPLICATION

PRAYER

JANUARY 4
DAY 4 OF 365

DEVOTIONAL

When the floods rose in Genesis 7-9, Noah trusted God's warning and built the ark. The Spirit that sustained him through waiting and uncertainty is the same Spirit who steadies us when life feels overwhelming. Even in judgment, God's mercy broke through in the rainbow—a covenant promise that His Word always holds true.

We see that same Spirit-empowered trust in Matthew 4, where Jesus stood against temptation. Instead of yielding to the enemy's lies, He believed His Father's word and declared it with power. From there, He called His disciples to follow Him, showing that belief is never passive—it demands obedience and surrender.

Proverbs 1 tells us that wisdom begins with the fear of the Lord. To believe is to revere His voice above all others, walking in truth that the Spirit makes alive within us.

Today, open your heart to the Spirit's guidance, trusting His voice to anchor you in storms and lead you in wisdom.

TODAY'S READINGS

GENESIS 7   GENESIS 8
GENESIS 9:1-17   MATTHEW 4:1-22   PROVERBS 1:1-7

JANUARY 4 | 21

S.O.A.P

SCRIPTURE

OBSERVATION

APPLICATION

PRAYER

JANUARY 5
DAY 5 OF 365

DEVOTIONAL

After the flood, humanity spread across the earth (Genesis 9:18-29; Genesis 10), but pride soon took over. In Genesis 11:1-9, people built the tower of Babel to make a name for themselves, and God scattered them in confusion. Pride divides, but faith trusts God's purpose.

Matthew 4:23-25 shows Jesus healing and proclaiming the kingdom, offering what human striving never could. In Matthew 5:1-20, He teaches that the blessed life flows from humility, mercy, purity, and righteousness. The Spirit forms these qualities in us so we can live as light in the world.

Psalm 4:1-8 ties it all together: peace is not found in striving and exalting oneself but in God's presence. He alone makes us dwell in safety.

Today, invite the Spirit to shape your heart after the ways of Jesus, trusting His kingdom way above your own.

TODAY'S READINGS

GENESIS 9:18-29   GENESIS 10   GENESIS 11:1-9
MATTHEW 4:23-25   MATTHEW 5:1-20   PSALM 4:1-8

S.O.A.P

SCRIPTURE

OBSERVATION

APPLICATION

PRAYER

JANUARY 6
DAY 6 OF 365

DEVOTIONAL

From Shem's line to Abram (Genesis 11:10-32), we believe God is writing a faithful story across generations. When the call came, Abram stepped out (Genesis 12) and later chose peace over striving with Lot, building altars as worship (Genesis 13). The same Spirit who stirs faith turns our steps toward trust, not self-promotion.

Jesus's teaching in Matthew 5:21-42 moves obedience from behavior to the heart—reconciling anger, guarding desire, speaking truth, laying down retaliation. Belief isn't box-checking; it's Spirit-empowered transformation that looks like everyday surrender.

Psalm 5 becomes our posture: morning prayer, "Lead me in Your righteousness," and confidence that His favor surrounds like a shield. Like Abram, we begin in worship and keep walking.

Today, take the next faithful step—pursue peace, tell the truth, reconcile quickly—trusting the Spirit to lead and God's favor to cover you.

TODAY'S READINGS

GENESIS 11:10-32   GENESIS 12   GENESIS 13
MATTHEW 5:21-42   PSALM 5:1-12

S.O.A.P

SCRIPTURE

OBSERVATION

APPLICATION

PRAYER

JANUARY 7
DAY 7 OF 365

DEVOTIONAL

Abram's story in Genesis 14-16 reminds us that faith trusts God's provision and protection. Even Hagar, cast aside, discovers the Lord as "the God who sees me" (Genesis 16:13). The Spirit assures us that no act of faith or cry of pain is hidden from Him, and His mercy reaches even those who feel forgotten. God is near in every circumstance.

Jesus's teaching in Matthew 5:43-48 and 6:1-24 calls us to live for the Father's eyes alone—loving enemies, giving, praying, and serving in secret. The Spirit shapes this hidden life of trust, freeing us from the weight of human approval and drawing us into deeper intimacy with the Father.

Psalm 6 echoes this hope: God hears the cries of the weary and answers with mercy. Belief clings to His presence, even in seasons of weakness.

Today, believe that the Father sees you fully, and let the Spirit shape your hidden life into worship.

TODAY'S READINGS

GENESIS 14   GENESIS 15   GENESIS 16
MATTHEW 5:43-48   MATTHEW 6:1-24   PSALM 6

S.O.A.P

SCRIPTURE

OBSERVATION

JANUARY 7 | **31**

APPLICATION

PRAYER

JANUARY 8
DAY 8 OF 365

DEVOTIONAL

In Genesis 17-18, God renews His covenant with Abram, promising a son when it seemed impossible. Abram believed, and even when Sarah laughed, the Spirit was at work, reminding them that nothing is too hard for the Lord. Faith looks beyond present limitations to trust the God who fulfills His word.

Jesus continues this call in Matthew 6:25-34 and 7:1-23, urging His followers not to be consumed with worry or judgment but to seek first the kingdom. Belief is more than reciting truth—it's Spirit-shaped dependence that trades anxiety for trust, self-righteousness for humility, and empty words for obedience.

Proverbs 1:18-19 warns that chasing greed or selfish gain ensnares those who pursue it. Belief chooses a different path: trusting God's provision instead of taking matters into our own hands.

Today, rest in the Spirit's assurance that God's promises are sure, His kingdom is worth seeking, and His provision is more than enough.

TODAY'S READINGS

**GENESIS 17   GENESIS 18   MATTHEW 6:25-34
MATTHEW 7:1-23   PROVERBS 1:18-19**

JANUARY 8 | 33

S.O.A.P

SCRIPTURE

OBSERVATION

APPLICATION

PRAYER

JANUARY 9

DAY 9 OF 365

DEVOTIONAL

Genesis 19-20 shows the fallout of unbelief as Lot's family struggles to leave Sodom and Abraham falters in fear. Yet God's mercy intervenes, pulling them out of destruction and preserving His covenant. Belief steadies us when fear tempts us to compromise, and the Spirit reminds us that God's faithfulness outlasts our failures.

Jesus illustrates this in Matthew 7:24-29 and 8:1-22. The wise builder who obeys His words, the leper healed by a touch, the centurion who trusted His authority—all reveal that true belief rests not in ourselves but in the word and power of Christ. When we submit to His authority, the Spirit works through us with unshakable strength.

Psalm 7:1-9 echoes this dependence: the righteous judge knows the heart and defends those who take refuge in Him. Belief declares that God alone is our shield.

Today, let the Spirit anchor your trust in Christ's authority, building your life on His Word and His strength.

TODAY'S READINGS

**GENESIS 19   GENESIS 20:1-18   MATTHEW 7:24-29
MATTHEW 8:1-22   PSALM 7:1-9**

S.O.A.P

SCRIPTURE

OBSERVATION

APPLICATION

PRAYER

JANUARY 10
DAY 10 OF 365

DEVOTIONAL

In Genesis 21-23, God fulfills His promise to Abraham and Sarah with the birth of Isaac, showing that no word from Him will fail. Even as Abraham walked through tests of faith, the Spirit enabled him to trust that God's covenant would endure. Belief holds fast even when the promise feels delayed or the path feels costly.

Matthew 8:23–34 and 9:1-13 reveal that same faithfulness in Jesus. He calms storms with a word, drives out demons with authority, forgives sins, and calls sinners to follow Him. We must cling to both His strength and His compassion.

Psalm 7:10-17 declares that God is the righteous judge and shield of those who trust Him. His justice and mercy flow together, covering those who believe.

Today, ask the Spirit to strengthen your trust in God's promises and anchor your heart in the faithfulness of Jesus.

TODAY'S READINGS

GENESIS 21   GENESIS 22   GENESIS 23
MATTHEW 8:23-34   MATTHEW 9:1-13   PSALM 7:10-17

S.O.A.P

SCRIPTURE

OBSERVATION

APPLICATION

PRAYER

JANUARY 11
DAY 11 OF 365

DEVOTIONAL

Genesis 24 shows how God faithfully directs those who seek Him. Abraham's servant prayed for a sign, and the Spirit led him straight to Rebekah—an answer that revealed God was already at work preparing the way.

That same truth unfolds in Matthew 9:14-38. Just as the servant was guided to Rebekah, Jesus sends His disciples into the harvest, reminding them that God is already at work drawing people to Himself. When you join Him where He leads, you can be confident that His Spirit equips you to carry His compassion into the world.

Psalm 8 anchors this with awe: the Creator who formed the heavens entrusts His people with His purposes. Belief holds this wonder—He is both majestic above all and near enough to guide our daily steps.

Today, ask the Spirit to direct your path and to open your eyes to where He is already at work.

TODAY'S READINGS

GENESIS 24   MATTHEW 9:14-38   PSALM 8

S.O.A.P

SCRIPTURE

OBSERVATION

APPLICATION

PRAYER

JANUARY 12
DAY 12 OF 365

DEVOTIONAL

In Genesis 25-26, Isaac learns that God's blessing is not bound by famine or conflict. Even when others opposed him, the Spirit led him to dig wells and find water where none was expected. God provides in every season, not by chance but by His covenant faithfulness.

Jesus echoes this in Matthew 10:1-31, sending out His disciples with authority but without extra supplies. Just as Isaac discovered God's provision in the land, the disciples were called to rely on the Spirit as they went. When we step out in obedience, we can be confident that the One who sends us will also sustain us.

Proverbs 1:20-33 warns of the danger of ignoring God's wisdom, yet offers security for those who listen. When you lean in to hear His voice, you'll find safety and peace in His guidance.

Today, trust the Spirit to provide what you need as you obey His call, knowing His wisdom and presence are enough.

TODAY'S READINGS

GENESIS 25   GENESIS 26   MATTHEW 10:1-31
PROVERBS 1:20-33

S.O.A.P

SCRIPTURE

OBSERVATION

APPLICATION

PRAYER

JANUARY 13
DAY 13 OF 365

DEVOTIONAL

In Genesis 27-28, Jacob's deception forces him into exile, yet in the wilderness, he encounters a vision of heaven open and a God who still promises to be with him. The Spirit meets us in the same way—reminding us that even in seasons of fear or failure, God's presence does not abandon us.

Jesus calls His followers to confess Him boldly and to embrace the cost of discipleship in Matthew 10 and 11, but He also affirms their worth—that even the smallest act done for Him is seen by the Father. With His presence, nothing surrendered is wasted.

Psalm 9:1-6 responds with worship, proclaiming the Lord as a refuge and the One who silences enemies. Our confidence rests not in ourselves but in the God who reigns and draws near.

Today, ask the Spirit to make you more aware of God's nearness, so you walk with courage and gratitude in whatever He calls you to.

TODAY'S READINGS

**GENESIS 27   GENESIS 28   MATTHEW 10:32-42
MATTHEW 11:1-15   PSALM 9:1-6**

S.O.A.P

SCRIPTURE

OBSERVATION

APPLICATION

PRAYER

JANUARY 14

DAY 14 OF 365

DEVOTIONAL

Genesis 29-30 shows Jacob caught in a cycle of striving—working for love, competing for favor, and chasing blessing. Yet even in the turmoil, God was faithful to His promise, building the family that would carry His covenant forward.

Jesus speaks directly to this in Matthew 11:16-30. Where people doubted His works, He called for faith that leads to rest: "Come to me, all you who are weary and burdened, and I will give you rest." True belief releases the need to prove ourselves and learns to trust His yoke, lightened by the Spirit's presence.

Psalm 9:7-12 confirms that trust: the Lord reigns forever, ruling with justice and remembering those who cry out in faith. He is both refuge and King, steadying all who look to Him.

Today, place your faith in the God who sees beyond your striving, and let the Spirit lead you into His rest.

TODAY'S READINGS

**GENESIS 29   GENESIS 30   MATTHEW 11:16-30
MATTHEW 9:7-12   PSALM 9:7-12**

S.O.A.P

SCRIPTURE

OBSERVATION

APPLICATION

PRAYER

JANUARY 15

DAY 15 OF 365

DEVOTIONAL

In Genesis 31, Jacob flees from Laban, uncertain of how things will unfold. Though deception and conflict marked their relationship, God protected Jacob and confirmed His covenant. Even when others act unjustly, the Spirit is present to guard and guide us.

Matthew 12:1-21 shows this more fully in Jesus. Confronted by critics, He revealed that true faith is not about rigid rule-keeping but about mercy and trust in God's heart. Quoting Isaiah, Matthew points to Christ as the servant who brings justice to the nations. He will not break the bruised reed.

Psalm 9:13-20 lifts our eyes to this same truth: the Lord remembers the oppressed, brings down the arrogant, and secures hope for those who trust Him. Faith holds steady, knowing His justice will prevail.

Today, put your confidence in Christ's mercy and the Spirit's presence, trusting that God is both your defender and your hope.

TODAY'S READINGS

GENESIS 31   MATTHEW 12:1-21
PSALM 9:13-20

S.O.A.P

SCRIPTURE

OBSERVATION

APPLICATION

PRAYER

JANUARY 16
DAY 16 OF 365

DEVOTIONAL

Genesis 32-33 tells of Jacob wrestling through the night, refusing to let go until he received a blessing. When morning came, he met Esau not with fear but with reconciliation. Belief looks like trusting the Spirit to transform even the most broken relationships.

In Matthew 12:22-45, Jesus reveals the true source of His power. While some accused Him of working by darkness, He declared that the Spirit of God was at work, bringing freedom and victory. We must discern the difference—trusting that God's kingdom is stronger than every chain and that His word will stand.

And in this power, he also grants wisdom to those who seek Him. Proverbs 2:1-11 reminds us that the Lord grants understanding, guards the paths of His people, and fills their hearts with knowledge and joy.

Today, hold fast to God in prayer, believe in the Spirit's power, and walk in the wisdom He freely gives.

TODAY'S READINGS

**GENESIS 32   GENESIS 33   MATTHEW 12:22-45
PROVERBS 2:1-11**

S.O.A.P

SCRIPTURE

OBSERVATION

APPLICATION

PRAYER

JANUARY 17
DAY 17 OF 365

DEVOTIONAL

Genesis 34-35 shows both the pain of human brokenness and the faithfulness of God's call. In the aftermath of violence, Jacob is told to return to build an altar to worship. Even when we are surrounded by sin and sorrow, faith turns back to God's presence.

In Matthew 12 and 13, Jesus deepens this truth, teaching that true family is found in those who hear and do the will of God. Through the parable of the sower, He reveals that belief takes root only in receptive hearts, where the Spirit brings life and fruitfulness.

Still, we may wrestle with what we see in the natural. Psalm 10:1-11 voices the cry of those who wonder why evil seems to prevail. God sees, hears, and knows the truth, and He will act in His time.

Today, ask the Spirit to make your heart good soil, ready to receive the Word and bear lasting fruit.

TODAY'S READINGS

**GENESIS 34   GENESIS 35   MATTHEW 12:46-50
MATTHEW 13:1-17   PSALM 10:1-11**

S.O.A.P

SCRIPTURE

OBSERVATION

APPLICATION

PRAYER

JANUARY 18
DAY 18 OF 365

DEVOTIONAL

Genesis 36-37 introduces Joseph, betrayed by his brothers and sold into slavery. What seemed like the end was really the beginning of God's larger plan. Even in loss, the Spirit reminds us to trust that His hand is still at work.

That hidden work is what Jesus describes in Matthew 13:18-35. Just as Joseph's suffering became seed for future redemption, the kingdom often begins small—like seed in the soil or yeast in the dough. Faith looks past what is visible and trusts the Spirit's quiet growth.

Psalm 10:12-18 reiterates this hope, assuring us that God hears the afflicted and strengthens those who wait for Him. His justice and purpose will stand.

Today, believe that what feels small or broken is part of God's greater plan, and let the Spirit steady your heart as you wait.

TODAY'S READINGS

GENESIS 36   GENESIS 37
MATTHEW 13:18-35   PSALM 10:12-18

S.O.A.P

SCRIPTURE

OBSERVATION

APPLICATION

PRAYER

JANUARY 19
DAY 19 OF 365

DEVOTIONAL

Genesis 38-39 places two stories side by side: Judah's sin that leads to shame, and Joseph's integrity that lands him in prison. Both remind us that human choices carry weight, yet the Spirit is present even in dark places, shaping God's purposes through brokenness and faithfulness alike.

Jesus explains this mystery in Matthew 13:36-58, teaching that the kingdom grows even as good and evil exist together until the final harvest. Like Joseph in prison, we may not see immediate results, but faith trusts that God's presence is steady and His purposes are unfolding.

Psalm 11 bridges these truths with confidence: though the foundations may seem shaken, the Lord remains on His throne. His eyes see clearly, and He upholds the righteous.

Today, rest in the Spirit's presence, believing that God is working even when circumstances feel uncertain or unjust.

TODAY'S READINGS

GENESIS 38   GENESIS 39   MATTHEW 13:36-58
PSALM 11

S.O.A.P

SCRIPTURE

OBSERVATION

APPLICATION

PRAYER

JANUARY 20
DAY 20 OF 365

DEVOTIONAL

In Genesis 40 and 41, Joseph waits in prison, forgotten by those he helped. Yet when Pharaoh dreams, the Spirit gives Joseph wisdom to interpret, and in a moment, he is lifted from the pit to a place of authority. God's timing is never late.

Matthew 14:1-21 shows this same truth in Jesus. Out of compassion, He feeds thousands with only five loaves and two fish. Just as Joseph trusted God's provision in Pharaoh's court, the disciples learned that little becomes much in the hands of the Lord.

As we give Him the little we have, Proverbs 2:12-22 reminds us that the wisdom we receive will keep us from paths that lead to ruin, guiding us into life. God's timing and provision are always aligned with His wisdom.

Today, trust the Spirit to sustain you in waiting, provide in scarcity, and lead you in wisdom until His purpose is revealed.

TODAY'S READINGS

GENESIS 40   GENESIS 41:1-40
MATTHEW 14:1-21   PROVERBS 2:12-22

JANUARY 20

S.O.A.P

SCRIPTURE

OBSERVATION

APPLICATION

PRAYER

JANUARY 21
DAY 21 OF 365

DEVOTIONAL

In Genesis 41:41-57 and 42, Joseph is lifted into authority and becomes the channel of provision during famine. The same brothers who betrayed him now stand before him in need. What once looked like loss is revealed as part of God's saving plan.

That same provision appears in Matthew 14:22-36 as Jesus walks on water and stills the disciples' fear. Just as Joseph's brothers were sustained in famine, the disciples were sustained in the storm, learning that faith means fixing our eyes on the One who holds every wave.

As we bring our need to Him, Matthew 15:1-9 and Psalm 12:1-8 warn us not to honor God with lips while our hearts are far away. Don't cling to empty words—cling to His.

Today, offer your need honestly to the Lord, and trust the Spirit to provide with wisdom, power, and faithfulness.

TODAY'S READINGS

GENESIS 41:41-57   GENESIS 42
MATTHEW 14:22-36   MATTHEW 15:1-9   PSALM 12:1-8

S.O.A.P

SCRIPTURE

OBSERVATION

APPLICATION

PRAYER

JANUARY 22
DAY 22 OF 365

DEVOTIONAL

In Genesis 43-44, Joseph's brothers return to Egypt, unaware of the mercy he is preparing to show them. Famine becomes the setting for repentance and reconciliation. The Spirit works through even painful seasons to soften hearts and draw people back to truth.

This same mercy is revealed in Matthew 15:10-39. Jesus teaches that purity flows not from outward rituals but from the heart, and then He demonstrates God's compassion by healing the sick and feeding thousands who have waited for deliverance.

Psalm 13 gives voice to the waiting heart: "How long, Lord?" Yet it ends with trust—"I will sing the Lord's praise, for he has been good to me." Mercy may not always come in the timing we expect, but faith holds to the God who never forgets.

Today, ask the Spirit to remind you of God's mercy and to shape your heart to extend that same mercy to others.

TODAY'S READINGS

**GENESIS 43   GENESIS 44
MATTHEW 15:10-39   PSALM 13**

JANUARY 22

S.O.A.P

SCRIPTURE

OBSERVATION

APPLICATION

PRAYER

JANUARY 23

DAY 23 OF 365

DEVOTIONAL

In Genesis 45-47:12, Joseph finally reveals himself to his brothers, not with vengeance but with grace: "God sent me ahead of you to preserve life." What they intended for harm, the Spirit had woven into a greater plan of salvation.

This same truth rises in Matthew 16:1-20. While the religious leaders demand signs, Peter confesses, "You are the Messiah, the Son of the living God." Just as Joseph's brothers struggled to recognize him, many failed to see Christ for who He was. But faith always recognizes God's plan unfolding in Jesus.

Psalm 14 laments the folly of those who deny God, yet declares that the Lord is present with the righteous. In every generation, His plan stands firm, and His people are never abandoned.

Today, trust the Spirit to open your eyes to God's greater plan, even when the path is hidden or the waiting is long.

TODAY'S READINGS

GENESIS 45   GENESIS 46
GENESIS 47:1-12   MATTHEW 16:1-20   PSALM 14

S.O.A.P

SCRIPTURE

OBSERVATION

APPLICATION

PRAYER

JANUARY 24
DAY 24 OF 365

DEVOTIONAL

In Genesis 47:13-31 and 48, Joseph provides for Egypt in famine while Jacob looks to the future, blessing his sons and passing on God's covenant promises. Even at the end of his life, Jacob's faith rested in what God had spoken, not just in what he could see.

That forward-looking faith is echoed in Matthew 16 and 17. Jesus speaks of His coming suffering, then reveals His glory on the mountaintop. Like Jacob blessing the next generation, the Father's voice declares, "This is my Son . . . listen to him."

Proverbs 3:1-10 draws it together, urging us to trust in the Lord with all our hearts and not lean on our own understanding. God's promises are sure, and His wisdom directs the way.

Today, let the Spirit strengthen your trust in both God's promises and His timing, as you walk in obedience and hope.

TODAY'S READINGS

**GENESIS 47:13-31   GENESIS 48   MATTHEW 16:21-28
MATTHEW 17:1-13   PROVERBS 3:1-10**

S.O.A.P

SCRIPTURE

OBSERVATION

APPLICATION

PRAYER

JANUARY 25
DAY 25 OF 365

DEVOTIONAL

In Genesis 49-50, Jacob blesses his sons and is laid to rest, and Joseph assures his brothers that their betrayal has been redeemed by God's hand. What began in sorrow ends in faith, declaring that God's purposes are greater than human failure.

Matthew 17 and 18 echo this call to trust. The disciples struggle with unbelief, yet Jesus shows that even faith as small as a mustard seed can move mountains. He teaches them to embrace humility like children and to cut off anything that leads them astray.

Psalm 15 ties these themes together with a picture of those who dwell in God's presence: those who walk with integrity, speak truth, and live faithfully. God is faithful to His people, and He calls His people to live in faithful trust toward Him.

Today, ask the Spirit to deepen your faith, turning small trust into strength and guiding you to walk faithfully before the Lord.

TODAY'S READINGS

**GENESIS 49   GENESIS 50   MATTHEW 17:14-27
MATTHEW 18:1-9   PSALM 15**

S.O.A.P

SCRIPTURE

OBSERVATION

APPLICATION

PRAYER

JANUARY 26
DAY 26 OF 365

DEVOTIONAL

Job 1-3 opens with a man who fears God yet loses nearly everything. In his grief, Job cries out with raw honesty, showing that faith is not silence in pain but a refusal to let go of God, even in unanswered questions.

In Matthew 18:10-35, Jesus tells of the shepherd who seeks one lost sheep and the king who forgives an unpayable debt. God's goodness is not abstract but deeply personal—He rescues, forgives, and calls us to extend the same mercy. Job's cries of suffering and Jesus's call to forgiveness both point us to a God who cares for the brokenhearted.

Psalm 16 ends today with confidence: "You make known to me the path of life; you will fill me with joy in your presence." Even in hardship, faith looks to the God who is near.

Today, let the Spirit anchor you in God's goodness, giving you courage to trust Him through both pain and mercy.

TODAY'S READINGS

JOB 1   JOB 2   JOB 3
MATTHEW 18:10-35   PSALM 16

S.O.A.P

SCRIPTURE

OBSERVATION

APPLICATION

PRAYER

JANUARY 27

DAY 27 OF 365

DEVOTIONAL

In Job 4-7, Job's friends offer explanations for his suffering, but their words only deepen his pain. Job insists on bringing his cries directly to God, showing us that real faith doesn't avoid questions but trusts that the Lord hears even in the midst of confusion.

That longing for God's nearness meets Jesus's teaching in Matthew 19:1-15. While others tried to restrict access to Him, Jesus welcomed children and blessed them. Just as Job poured out his heart, believing God would listen, Christ assures us that the Father's heart is open to the humble and the dependent.

Psalm 17:1-5 echoes this confidence: God hears the righteous cry and holds their steps secure. Our prayers are never wasted, and our lives are guarded by His hand.

Today, trust the Spirit to remind you that God hears every cry and delights in drawing near to those who come to Him with childlike faith.

TODAY'S READINGS

JOB 4   JOB 5   JOB 6   JOB 7
MATTHEW 19:1-15   PSALM 17:1-5

S.O.A.P

SCRIPTURE

OBSERVATION

APPLICATION

PRAYER

JANUARY 28
DAY 28 OF 365

DEVOTIONAL

In Job 8-10, Job wrestles with God's justice. His friends insist suffering must be punishment, but Job refuses their easy answers. Instead, he longs for someone to plead his case before God. He doesn't ignore hard questions but clings to the Spirit's assurance that God is righteous even when life feels unfair.

That same struggle appears in Matthew 19:16-30, when the rich young ruler seeks eternal life but walks away unwilling to surrender. Jesus shows that righteousness is not earned by effort or wealth but received through wholehearted trust.

Proverbs 3:11-20 connects these truths: God's discipline is not rejection but love, shaping us through wisdom so we may walk in life. The One who founded the earth by wisdom is faithful to guide His people in every generation.

Today, ask the Spirit to help you trust God's righteousness, even when His ways stretch beyond your understanding.

TODAY'S READINGS

JOB 8   JOB 9   JOB 10
MATTHEW 19:16-30   PROVERBS 3:11-20

JANUARY 28 | 93

S.O.A.P

SCRIPTURE

OBSERVATION

APPLICATION

PRAYER

JANUARY 29
DAY 29 OF 365

DEVOTIONAL

In Job 11-14, Job pushes back against his friends' shallow answers and wrestles with the mystery of God's ways. He acknowledges that life is fragile and full of questions, yet he clings to the hope that wisdom belongs to God alone.

Matthew 20:1-19 carries this theme forward in Jesus's parable of the vineyard workers. To some, the master's generosity seemed unfair, but His wisdom overturned their expectations. Just as Job learned that God's ways cannot be reduced to human logic, Jesus shows that grace cannot be measured by our standards.

Psalm 17:6-12 becomes the prayer of those who believe: "I call on you, my God, for you will answer me." When life feels unjust, we rest in the wisdom and mercy of the One who sees clearly and answers faithfully.

Today, ask the Spirit to deepen your trust in God's wisdom, even when His ways stretch beyond your understanding.

TODAY'S READINGS

**JOB 11   JOB 12   JOB 13
JOB 14   MATTHEW 20:1-19   PSALM 17:6-12**

S.O.A.P

SCRIPTURE

OBSERVATION

APPLICATION

PRAYER

JANUARY 30
DAY 30 OF 365

DEVOTIONAL

In Job 15-18, Job's friends grow harsher in their accusations, but Job continues to cry out to God in his weakness. His honesty shows that faith is not pretending to be strong but depending on the One who is. The Spirit meets us in our frailty—God's strength is made perfect in our weakness.

This truth is found in Matthew 20:20-34. While the disciples sought position and power, Jesus taught that greatness comes through serving. Then, in compassion, He restored sight to two blind men who called out for mercy.

The overall message? The Lord delivers His people and satisfies them with His presence (Psalm 17:13-15). In a world that exalts power, faith rests in the strength that only God provides.

Today, ask the Spirit to exchange your weakness for His strength and to shape you into a servant who reflects Christ.

TODAY'S READINGS

JOB 15   JOB 16   JOB 17   JOB 18
MATTHEW 20:20-34   PSALM 17:13-15

JANUARY 30

S.O.A.P

SCRIPTURE

OBSERVATION

APPLICATION

PRAYER

JANUARY 31

DAY 31 OF 365

DEVOTIONAL

In Job 19-21, Job endures accusations yet makes one of the clearest declarations of faith: "I know that my Redeemer lives, and that in the end he will stand on the earth." Even in suffering, he looks forward to God's salvation.

That same hope unfolds in Matthew 21:1-17, as Jesus enters Jerusalem to shouts of "Hosanna!" The crowds longed for deliverance, and though they misunderstood how it would come, God's salvation had arrived in Christ. Job's cry for a Redeemer meets its answer in Jesus, the King who brings life.

The parallel is obvious: God is our strength, our rock, and our deliverer who hears our cries (Psalm 18:1-6). Salvation is not an idea but a living reality in the God who saves.

Today, lift your voice in trust that your Redeemer lives, and allow the Spirit to fill you with hope in His salvation.

TODAY'S READINGS

JOB 19   JOB 20   JOB 21
MATTHEW 21:1-17   PSALM 18:1-6

S.O.A.P

SCRIPTURE

OBSERVATION

APPLICATION

PRAYER

www.ingramcontent.com/pod-product-compliance
Lightning Source LLC
Chambersburg PA
CBHW070206100426
42743CB00013B/3070

Belief declares that God alone is our shield.

Every sunrise whispers, Begin again. January reminds us that God is still in the business of beginnings—turning chaos into creation and despair into hope. From Genesis to Matthew, each page calls us to believe again: to trust His voice over fear and His promises over the past.

In We Believe by Gary Lewis, January lays the foundation for a year of faith-filled reading through Scripture. Each day walks you through creation, the first steps of faith, and the gospel's opening chapters to reveal what belief truly means: complete trust in the One who makes all things new.

You will:

- Rediscover the power of beginnings and the God who still creates.
- Learn to anchor your life in God's Word instead of circumstances.
- See how belief and obedience are inseparable acts of worship.
- Develop a daily rhythm of Scripture engagement.
- Experience renewed hope from the God who redeems every start.

The year begins with belief—because faith in God isn't a resolution; it's a revolution—of the heart.

Bishop Gary J. Lewis serves as general overseer for the Church of God. He has ministered as a student pastor, senior pastor, state youth and discipleship director, assistant and director of International Youth and Discipleship, state administrative bishop, and member of the International Executive Council (Council of 18). Bishop Lewis is a gifted administrator and anointed leader with a clear message for the church today.